TRUE-LIFE MONSTERS OF THE PREHISTORIC SEAS

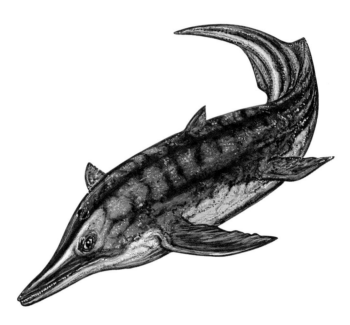

For a free color catalog describing Gareth Stevens' list of high-quality books and multimedia programs, call 1-800-542-2595 (USA) or 1-800-461-9120 (Canada). Gareth Stevens Publishing's Fax: (414) 225-0377.

Library of Congress Cataloging-in-Publication Data

Fisher, Enid.
    True-life monsters of the prehistoric seas/by Enid Fisher; illustrated
by Richard Grant.
        p. cm. — (World of dinosaurs)
    Includes bibliographical references and index.
    Summary: Describes various prehistoric sea creatures that lived at
the same time as the dinosaurs, including the placodus, mosasaurus,
and plesiosaurus.
    ISBN 0-8368-2293-5 (lib. bdg.)
    1. Marine animals, Fossil—Juvenile literature. [1. Marine animals,
Fossil. 2. Prehistoric animals.] I. Grant, Richard, 1959- ill.
II. Title. III. Series: World of dinosaurs.
QE851.F54   1999
567'.09162—dc21   98-45733

This North American edition first published in 1999 by
Gareth Stevens Publishing
1555 North RiverCenter Drive, Suite 201
Milwaukee, Wisconsin 53212 USA

This U.S. edition © 1999 by Gareth Stevens, Inc.
Created with original © 1998 by Quartz Editorial Services,
112 Station Road, Edgware HA8 7AQ U.K.
Additional end matter © 1999 by Gareth Stevens, Inc.

Consultant: Dr. Paul Barrett, Paleontologist, Specialist in Biology and
  Evolution of Dinosaurs, University of Cambridge, England.

Printed in Mexico

1 2 3 4 5 6 7 8 9 03 02 01 00 99

TRUE-LIFE MONSTERS OF THE PREHISTORIC SEAS

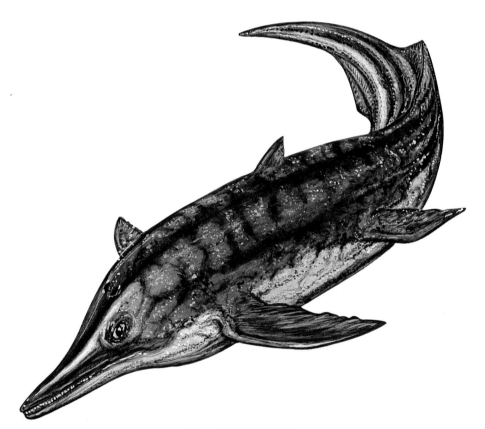

by Enid Fisher
Illustrations by Richard Grant

Gareth Stevens Publishing
MILWAUKEE

CONTENTS

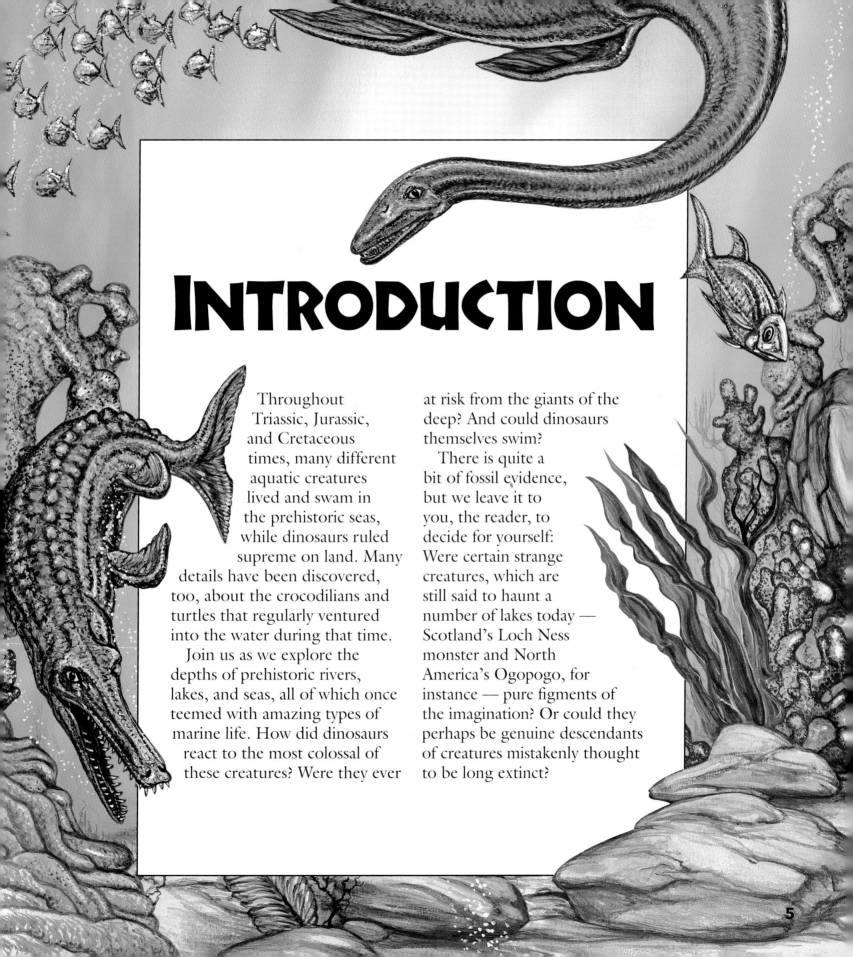

INTRODUCTION

Throughout Triassic, Jurassic, and Cretaceous times, many different aquatic creatures lived and swam in the prehistoric seas, while dinosaurs ruled supreme on land. Many details have been discovered, too, about the crocodilians and turtles that regularly ventured into the water during that time.

Join us as we explore the depths of prehistoric rivers, lakes, and seas, all of which once teemed with amazing types of marine life. How did dinosaurs react to the most colossal of these creatures? Were they ever at risk from the giants of the deep? And could dinosaurs themselves swim?

There is quite a bit of fossil evidence, but we leave it to you, the reader, to decide for yourself: Were certain strange creatures, which are still said to haunt a number of lakes today — Scotland's Loch Ness monster and North America's Ogopogo, for instance — pure figments of the imagination? Or could they perhaps be genuine descendants of creatures mistakenly thought to be long extinct?

COULD DINOSAURS SWIM?

Fossilized dinosaur footprints in rocks that were also imprinted with ripples washed on to some prehistoric shores. This indicates that they were not afraid to get their feet wet, but could they swim?

The sauropod was now chest high in cool water. Hungry, it had spied a small island in the middle of the lake that was covered with lush foliage and had paced the shoreline for a convenient spot to wade in. Soon, the lapping waters began to lift its massive bulk, pitching its body forward so that its hind legs left the safety of firm ground. With its neck outstretched, the great creature could now float easily on the swell, while a few sideways flexings of its awesome tail would propel it forward. In just a few minutes, it would reach the shallows again and walk out toward the mouth-watering feast ahead.

Experts studying tracks left by giant sauropods in what is now the Dry Mesa Quarry in Texas — which was only a coastal region in Jurassic times — believe these creatures frequently crossed the narrow stretches of water in the search for food. Uneven prints in what would have been the bed of large lakes also confirm that forelimbs were used like barge poles to steer the sauropods along. Other species of dinosaurs also went into the water. The duck-billed hadrosaurs of Cretaceous times, for example, paddled in shallows, sucking up underwater foliage in their wide mouths. Experts conclude from irregular fossilized prints, such as those found in the Peace River region of the United States, that the hadrosaurs also left the safety of dry land for richer pickings.

These dinosaurs seem to have traveled through the water by bouncing at intervals from one hind leg to the other. Indeed, the Peace River trackways show only the front parts of the feet, indicating that their owners did not walk through the water but pushed themselves along while floating. Their rigid tails and strong back muscles, too, would have helped keep the creatures buoyant, while they probably struck out in dog-paddle movements with their forelimbs, much as horses, deer, and even elephants and rhinoceroses do today.

However, it is highly unlikely that dinosaurs ever embarked on voyages over vast oceans. Any swimming abilities they may have had were confined to local areas and were severely limited.

PRESENTING THE PLACODONTS

Although not entirely aquatic, placodonts seem to have spent a great deal of time in the water. Here, with the help of their powerful jaws and teeth, they would feast on the millions of mollusks that encrusted the prehistoric seabeds.

With the hot Triassic sun barely visible in the murky, shallow water, **Placodus** was unable to see clearly. It had to feel its way along the rocky seafloor. Instinctively, it now and then opened its wide mouth and ripped shellfish from their moorings. Its blunt, flat, back teeth would grind the shells into a mush, and **Placodus** would satisfy its hunger for a while.

Placodonts (the name means "plate-toothed") were some of the first reptiles to move into the water during Triassic times. However, they were not really built for life adrift. Their limbs, although useful for steering through the water, were better suited to hauling their 6.5 foot (2-meter)-long bodies over land. They traveled this way alongside long-necked, long-tailed nothosaurs at particular times — to lay eggs, for example. But the seas always beckoned when hunger struck, because a placodont's staple diet was shellfish, such as clams and mussels.

Tough teeth

Once in the water, a placodont would propel itself along with its four limbs. Then, with its shovel-shaped snout held rigidly in front of its body, it used its six sharp front teeth to pluck prey from the seabed, which it swallowed whole. The hungry placodont would then grind together the fourteen flattened teeth that covered the roof and floor of its mouth to crack the mollusks and release their contents.

Some placodonts, such as **Placodus**, were soft-bodied, so they may have been easy prey for land- or water-based predators. Others, however — such as tough **Psephoderma** — were covered with scaly body armor that looked very much like a turtle's shell and is known as a carapace. This would have been their only protection against attack by a predator, since they were not equipped to fight back and were probably much too heavy to flee from danger.

Placodonts were plentiful in the European Triassic seas; in fact, several fossils have been dug up in what is now Italy. They did not adapt to changing conditions and became extinct at the end of the Triassic era, some 213 million years ago.

It also remains a mystery why no other placodont remains have been unearthed in other parts of the world. They may have been exclusive to what are now European waters. Perhaps they will one day be found elsewhere.

MEET THE MOSASAURS

With long jaws full of sharp, spiked teeth, mosasaurs were quick to attack, and probably even fought among themselves over territory and mates.

Balloons of blood clouded the already turbulent waters as two mosasaurs thrashed around in a vain attempt to escape each other's vicious jaws. The larger beast, which lived in that particular stretch of Cretaceous ocean, grimly held on to the intruder's tail. Desperate now, the interloper flexed its muscular body one more time. The jerking loosened its assailant's grip just long enough for it to slither away to safer feeding grounds.

Mosasaurs were extremely territorial and would fight to the death over a stretch of water. These massive sea lizards would also prey on other marine creatures for food. When they were around, nothing was safe. What a frightening sight **Mosasaurus** must have presented!

The jaws of a mosasaur had rows of backward-leaning, pointed teeth that were ideal for tearing flesh and were set into a thick, solid head. Behind this stretched a muscular body and a flattened, blunt tail, which the creature flexed to propel itself through the water. Flippers also helped steer it quickly in whichever direction it chose, despite its great size.

Marine monsters

Most fossilized remains show that mosasaurs grew up to 15-30 feet (4.5-9 m) long, but some of the forty known species, such as **Tylosaurus**, found in Kansas, grew to 40 feet (12 m). Tylosaurus remains have also been found in New Zealand.

The longest mosasaur skeleton — belonging to a **Hainosaurus** — was discovered in Belgium. This skeleton was an astounding 56 feet (17 m) in length!

Although mosasaurs were reptiles, they had long since lost the ability to survive on land. This meant that they could not leave the water to lay eggs. Instead, experts believe, the females kept their eggs inside their bodies and then delivered live young, like some species of snakes do today.

Mosasaurs became extinct at the same time as the dinosaurs, about 65 million years ago. One mosasaur relative lives on today, however, in the form of the monitor lizard, a completely land-based creature that inhabits tropical regions of Earth.

RIBBON REPTILES

The largest creatures ever to populate the oceans were the plesiosaurs, prehistoric reptiles that swam in Earth's seas for over 100 million years.

The monster **Plesiosaurus** looked around nervously. The Jurassic seaways could be dangerous when vicious predators, such as **Ichthyosaurus**, were around — even more so when newly-hatched infants were making their first trip into the water. Soon after breaking out of eggs that had been laid in the sand and covered by the mother, the clutch of youngsters began to slither awkwardly down to the sea. Here, they would start their search for a meal of fish.

Although plesiosaurs lived in the water much of the time, they dragged themselves to land to lay their eggs. This was not an easy task for these large creatures. Their barrel-shaped bodies were a dead weight on land, although their four flipper-like limbs, which they used to power themselves in the water, were handy for digging nesting places.

Plesiosaurs were such different creatures when in water! They would flap their flippers up and down like wings, rather than backward and forward like oars, and plow smoothly through the seas. They accomplished this in spite of their great weight, which could be up to one ton. At the same time, they would use their extremely long, flexible necks — which were sometimes over half their total body length of 10-13 feet (3-4 m) — and their short, sturdy snouts, to search all around for a likely meal.

Plesiosaurs usually ate fish or squid, catching the prey as they swam past by lashing out with their necks at lightning speed. The plesiosaurs trapped their prey in jaws that were lined with sharp, interlocking teeth.

Up for air

Although completely at home in the sea, plesiosaurs could not breathe under water; they had to come up for air. They needed to do this frequently since their lungs were small. In fact, experts claim that larger lungs filled with air would almost certainly have caused these great creatures to float to the surface, and they

would have been unable to dive for food or defend themselves.

As it was, plesiosaurs were prime targets for hungry, seagoing predators, such as their close relatives, the vicious, razor-toothed pliosaurs, and the dolphin-like ichthyosaurs. Plesiosaurs had no defense weapons. For example, they could not lash out with their tails and were not quick enough in the water to make an escape.

Nevertheless, these awesome creatures managed to survive for 100 million years. They were direct descendants of the smaller Triassic nothosaurs. **Pistosaurus,** the first of the species, was 10 feet (3 m) long and appeared in the oceans in Early Jurassic times, about 200 million years ago. By Cretaceous times, they were truly

monstrous; many were over 40 feet (12 m) long. In fact, the largest fossil bones unearthed so far are of a creature scientists call **Elasmosaurus,** or "ribbon reptile," which reached a length of 46 feet (14 m). This included 20-23 feet (6-7 m) of neck!

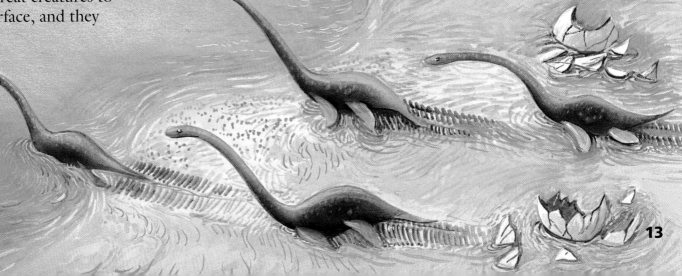

TERROR OF THE DEEP

One of the most feared creatures in the prehistoric seas was the pliosaur — a short-bodied, bullet-headed relative of the plesiosaur. Most other ocean-dwellers lived in terror of its slashing jaws.

Kronosaurus was making good progress through the murky seas. With jaws wide open, it scooped up large numbers of fish as it sliced through the deep waters. An unsuspecting plesiosaur lay ahead, trying to catch a fish. That would make a much more substantial meal for this monstrous sea reptile! Kronosaurus would soon go in for the kill.

The mightiest of the pliosaurs, Kronosaurus was the tyrant of the southern seas — where the continent of Australia is located today — for 130 million years, from Early Jurassic times right through to Late Cretaceous times. It was named for the god Cronos, or Kronos, from Greek mythology. From fossils found in Queensland, Australia, scientists estimate that this creature was a staggering 56 feet (17 m) in length. Its head was 8 feet (2.4 m) long — the height from floor to ceiling in an average house. Most of it was taken up by cavernous jaws lined with closely packed, backward-curving teeth. Pliosaurs were built for attacking and tearing at prey, much like today's killer whales, although they are not related. Pliosaurus, reaching a length of 22 feet (6.7 m), would even confront the much-larger, dolphin-like ichthyosaurs — often 48 feet (14.6 m) in length! Some smaller pliosaurs, such as Peloneustes in what is now Western Europe, however, may have been content simply to cruise along and bite chunks out of passing squid.

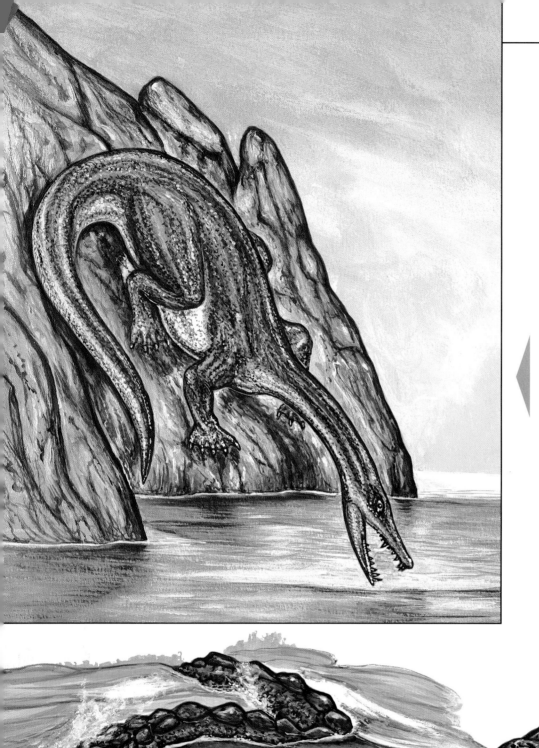

Nothosaurus

This Triassic creature had a long neck and long feet that could be used as paddles. Although **Nothosaurus** (<u>NOH</u>-THOH-<u>SAW</u>-RUS) spent a lot of time in the sea, it could also come out on to land. It lived on a diet of fish.

Proterosuchus

An early archosaur, **Proterosuchus** (PROH-<u>TERR</u>-OH-<u>SOOK</u>-US) was 5 feet (1.5 m) long and swam in the Triassic seas. It also climbed on land using its sprawling limbs and chased smaller reptilians, which it devoured greedily.

TRIASSIC SEAS

▶ **Tanistropheus**
Remains show that **Tanistropheus**
(TAN-ISS-TROFF-EE-US) had a very
long neck. This was certainly a
useful asset for hauling in fish
when not actually in the water but
resting on a rock. In fact, its neck
has even been compared to an
expandable fishing rod.

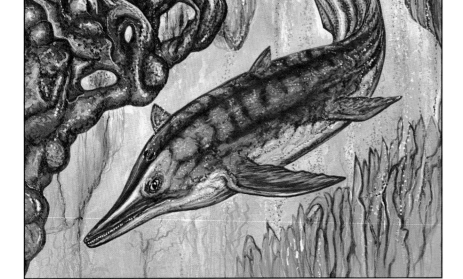

Mixosaurus
Like all the ichthyosaurs, **Mixosaurus** (MIX-OH-SAW-RUS)
had a dolphin-shaped body, small flippers, a fishlike
tail, and no distinct neck. It has been unearthed
in Europe and may have grown to 40 feet
(12 m) in length. Ichthyosaurs gave birth
to live young.

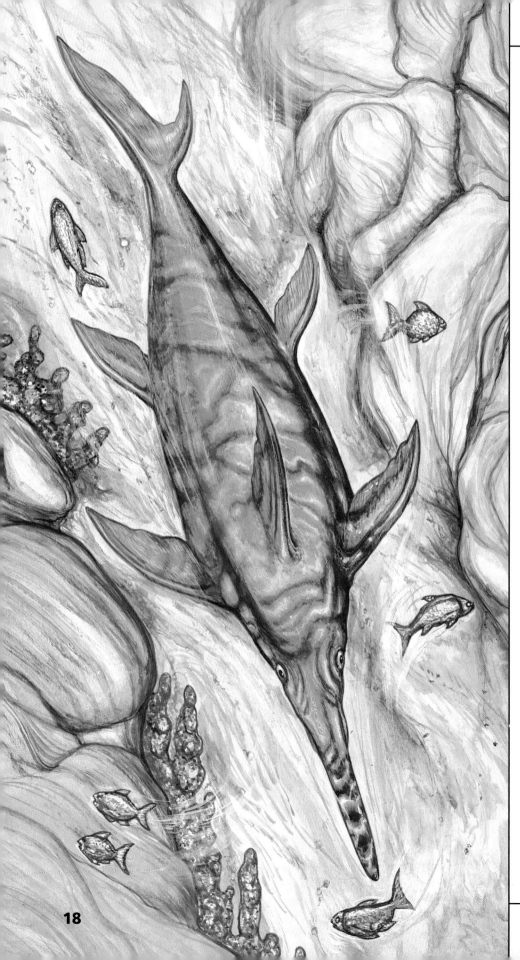

IN THE

Eurhinosaurus

The sea creature **Eurhinosaurus** (YOUR-<u>IN</u>-OH-<u>SAW</u>-RUS) was dolphin-shaped, like all ichthyosaurs, but had an extraordinarily long snout. Its remains have been found in Europe.

Ammonites

Resembling today's mollusks but often larger, **ammonites** are the most numerous fossils of Triassic times and the whole Mesozoic era.

Dapedium

The **Dapedium** (DAP-<u>EE</u>-DEE-UM) was a fairly common fish by Jurassic times. It was not very large and had a bony skeleton with a characteristic gaping mouth and rounded, deep body.

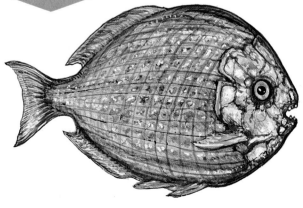

JURASSIC SEAS

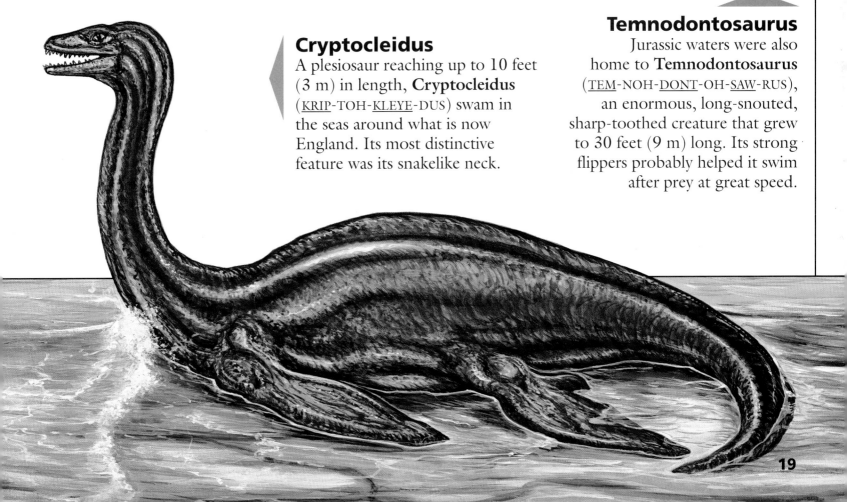

Cryptocleidus
A plesiosaur reaching up to 10 feet (3 m) in length, **Cryptocleidus** (<u>KRIP</u>-TOH-<u>KLEYE</u>-DUS) swam in the seas around what is now England. Its most distinctive feature was its snakelike neck.

Temnodontosaurus
Jurassic waters were also home to **Temnodontosaurus** (<u>TEM</u>-NOH-<u>DONT</u>-OH-<u>SAW</u>-RUS), an enormous, long-snouted, sharp-toothed creature that grew to 30 feet (9 m) long. Its strong flippers probably helped it swim after prey at great speed.

IN THE CRETACEOUS SEAS

Muraeonosaurus

A typical plesiosaur, **Muraeonosaurus** (<u>MUHR</u>-EYE-<u>ON</u>-OH-<u>SAW</u>-RUS) had a long neck and four powerful flippers. It could swim under water, but still needed to come up and fill its lungs with air.

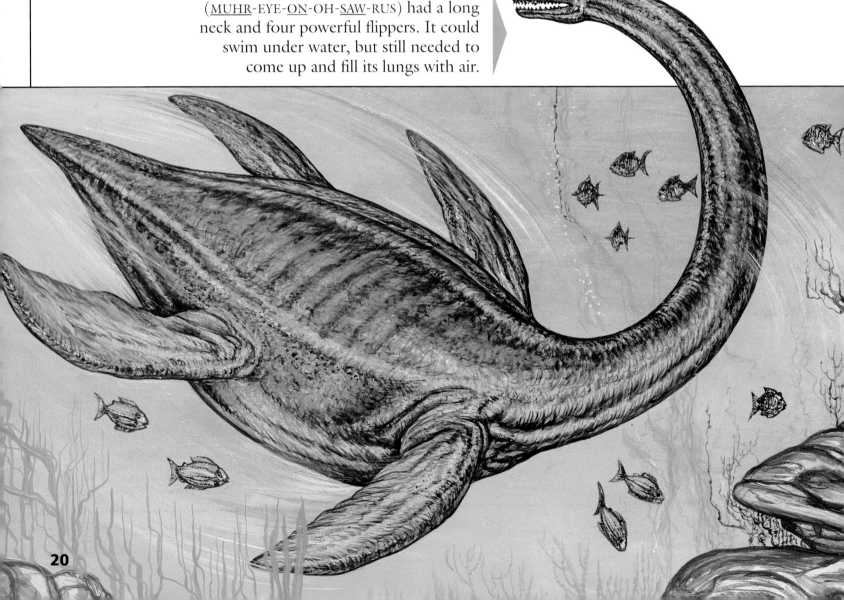

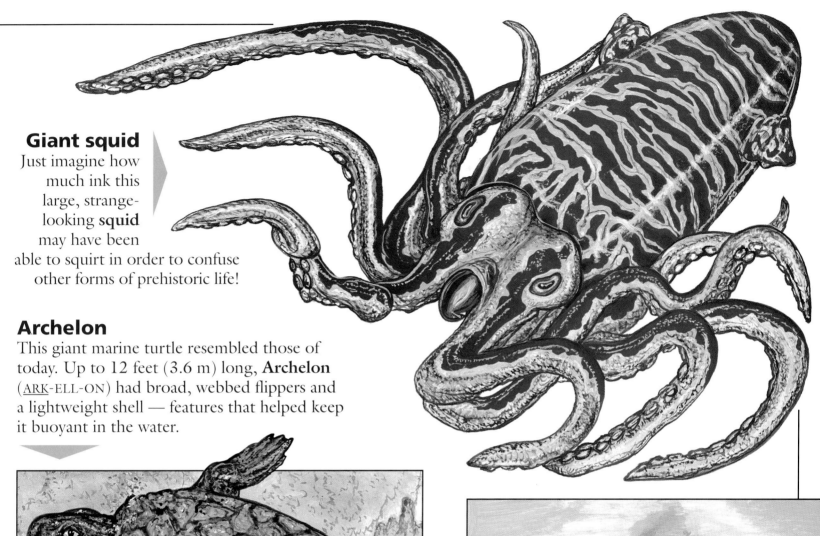

Giant squid
Just imagine how much ink this large, strange-looking **squid** may have been able to squirt in order to confuse other forms of prehistoric life!

Archelon
This giant marine turtle resembled those of today. Up to 12 feet (3.6 m) long, **Archelon** (ARK-ELL-ON) had broad, webbed flippers and a lightweight shell — features that helped keep it buoyant in the water.

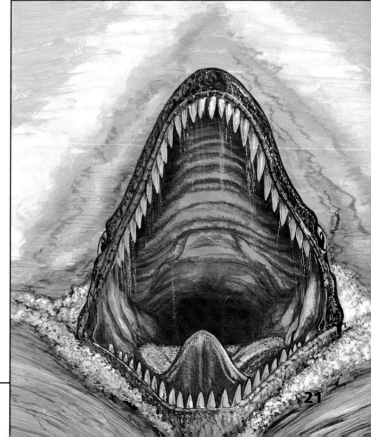

Phobosuchus
A crocodilian with a huge mouth, **Phobosuchus** (FOH-BOH-SOOK-US) grew as long as 50 feet (15 m). Many dinosaur species may have found it a fearful predator.

21

EVIDENCE OF DISASTER

Ichthyosaurs, such as Shonisaurus, were superbly adapted to the water and never came out of it. At times, however, they beached themselves and brought about certain death.

The scene was an eerie one. No sound but the wind whipping the sand disturbed the lonely Cretaceous shore, as row upon row of **Shonisaurus** lay motionless on the beach. One by one, they had come ashore, moving on the shallow waters until their massive bodies finally became completely beached.

Their fossilized remains have been uncovered in Nevada. But why would these mighty sea monsters have left the water in this way? So far, no one has been

them to come out of the water, because this species of marine reptile was totally adapted to life in the sea.

Like all ichthyosaurs, **Shonisaurus** had powerful flippers, and its body was long and streamlined — perfect for slicing through the water. A massive tail fluke, which could be flicked horizontally back and forth, enabled it to swim at

able to offer a satisfactory explanation. Perhaps, some experts conclude, the **Shonisaurus** beached themselves for no accountable cause, just as whales have been known to do in modern times. There was no obvious reason for

dined mainly on shell-dwelling, squid-like creatures, such as **ammonite**s and belemnites. One fossilized skeleton had the remains of 1,600 of these in its stomach cavity!

Most ichthyosaurs were a lot smaller than the prey they attacked; many species were only about 13-16 feet (4-4.8 m) long. **Shonisaurus** was a giant among them, reaching lengths of up to 50 feet (15 m). Even so, it was completely at ease in the water, and rarely left it, making the fossilized evidence for beaching all the more mysterious.

Although ichthyosaurs lived for many millions of years, from the Triassic right through the Jurassic and halfway through the Cretaceous era, the species was in decline for much of that time. Perhaps, like other prehistoric creatures, such as the pterosaurs, ichthyosaurs were simply too specialized to survive the environmental changes that were engulfing Earth.

speeds up to 30 miles (48 kilometers) per hour. This allowed it to outpace any other sea-dweller. Most of its aquatic companions, such as the plesiosaurs, pliosaurs, and early sharks, were fair game for a creature with such menacing jaws. Its cone-shaped, ridged teeth were clearly built for tearing out a chunk of flesh in seconds. Ichthyosaurs, however,

PREHISTORIC CROCODILES

Not all prehistoric creatures disappeared from Earth millions of years ago. In fact, the crocodiles and alligators that live in the world's tropical rivers and lakes today have not changed much since Triassic times.

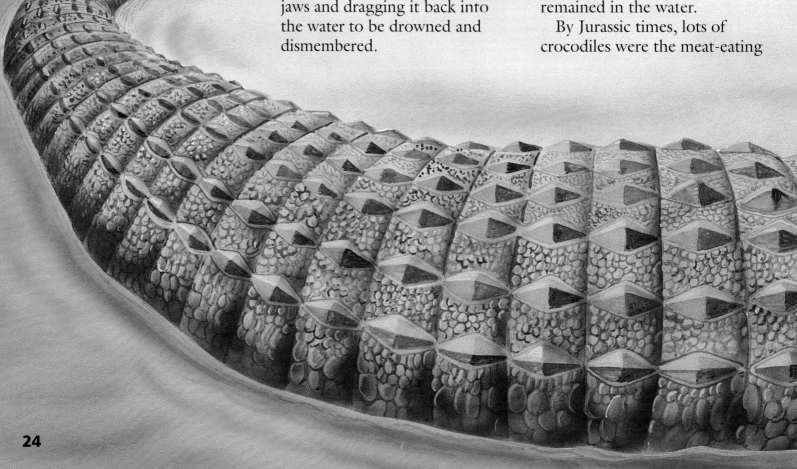

Phobosuchus, a gigantic crocodile, lay quietly in the water. Only its eyes and gaping jaws betrayed its presence in the shallow Cretaceous seas that covered what is now Texas. It had lined up its next meal — an unsuspecting sauropod that was browsing along the shoreline. Soon, **Phobosuchus** would launch itself at its prey, clamping the threshing body in its strong jaws and dragging it back into the water to be drowned and dismembered.

Experts believe it was the failure of the small, early, land-based crocodiles to compete with larger species, such as the emerging dinosaurs, that drove them into the water. Once there, they found plentiful food in the form of fish and other small creatures, and remained in the water.

By Jurassic times, lots of crocodiles were the meat-eating

creatures they are today. In fact, two fossilized crocodile skeletons, found among the remains of several **Iguanodon** in Europe, lead experts to believe they were capable, like modern crocodiles, of taking on creatures much larger than themselves. **Phobosuchus** certainly survived on a diet that included hadrosaurs and sauropods, which it caught when they were busy browsing in the shallows for plants.

Fish-eaters

Not all Jurassic crocodilians were meat-eaters, however. **Metriorhynchus** (whose Jurassic fossils have been found in today's Europe and South America) and **Geosaurus** ate fish and evolved to follow an almost totally aquatic lifestyle. Their bodies shed the armor plating, the limbs became rounded, and the tail became curved, like a fin. Unfortunately, such modifications did not guarantee permanent survival, and these sea crocodiles became extinct before the close of the Jurassic era.

PLESIOSAUR DISCOVERY

The very first plesiosaur remains were discovered by fifteen-year-old Mary Anning in the chalky cliffs around her home in Lyme Regis, England, in 1814. This area is still a rich fossil-hunting ground for amateurs and experts.

Measuring about 16 feet (4.8 m) in length, the plesiosaur, *below*, must have been a magnificent creature in its time.

Our knowledge that such creatures really did inhabit the seas hundreds of millions of years ago may not have come about so early if there had not been

a craze for collecting fossils among the upper classes in eighteenth-century Europe.

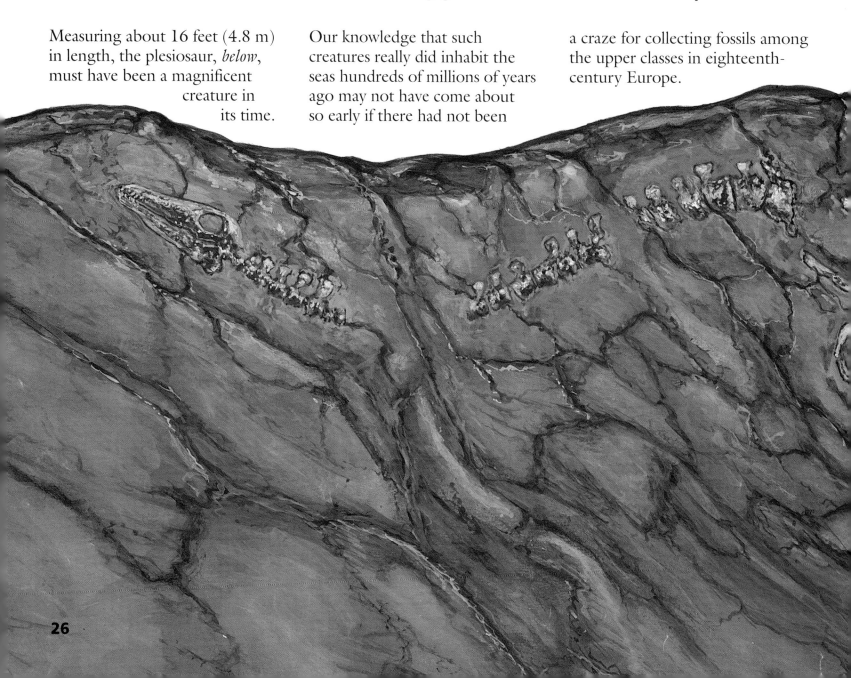

They relied on local people to find the fossils and paid handsomely for whatever specimens appeared. Mary Anning's father made a living selling fossils, and, when he died, the family carried on the trade. The plesiosaur was not Mary's first major discovery. When only eleven years old, in 1810, she discovered a bone from what was to be the first ichthyosaur skeleton ever found and sold it for £23 (about $40) — worth as much as £1000 ($1,700) in today's money. A few years later, she sold the plesiosaur remains for four times as much.

Collecting fossils was not just a money-making exercise for Mary Anning. She devoted her life not only to locating possible finds, but also to developing methods of their extraction from rock without ruining them. She seemed able to detect the presence of a substantial fossil collection from just a small bump in a particular rock. She could also piece together the bones in the correct order, in spite of no formal training in the science of paleontology.

By 1830, Mary had unearthed three complete ichthyosaurs and two plesiosaurs. These, together with many other examples of fossils, made up her impressive collection. The area around Lyme Regis continues to yield important discoveries today. Local amateurs still chisel rocks from the cliffs and treat them chemically until all the fossils are exposed, ready for examination.

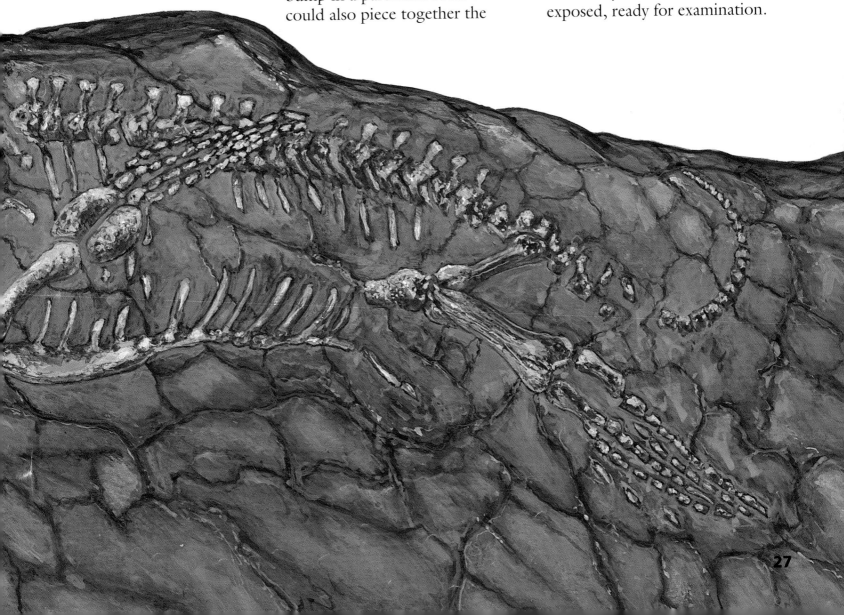

PREHISTORIC SURVIVORS?

Some creatures alive today — turtles and crocodiles, for instance —
had ancestors that lived with the dinosaurs. If these species have survived,
is it possible that others also defied extinction and continue to live
in remote, watery hideouts in certain regions of the world?

The waters of Lake Okanagan, in British Columbia, Canada, were chilly, even though it was the middle of summer. What sent an even greater chill down the spine of the intrepid swimmer, however, was the sensation of being pushed around by a long, muscular shape that passed by in a matter of seconds. Suddenly, in the distance ahead, three or four fleshy coils, each about 16 feet (4.8 m) across, appeared above the surface, undulating unnervingly through the water.

If the swimmer can be believed, this was an encounter with a sea-dweller known locally for hundreds of years as Ogopogo. Several other sightings have also occurred; witnesses claim that Ogopogo is gray in color, with a snakelike body and whalelike flukes at the end of its tail. Other creatures of similar build have been sighted in lakes all over the world, such as Lake Van in Turkey and Lake Ikeda in Japan. Japanese mothers to this day do not allow their children to play in the lake, for fear of meeting the creature they call *Issie*.

Alive and well?

Scientists called cryptozoologists dismiss explanations that these sightings are no more than ripples on the water made by the wind or passing motorboats. They claim that they are true sightings of creatures that supposedly died out millions of years ago. Intriguingly, fossil remains of some prehistoric sea creatures do bear a close resemblance to descriptions of the elusive beast called Ogopogo.

Several sightings on vast and lonely lakes have led cryptozoologists to believe that plesiosaurs are possibly still alive and well. The "monsters" sighted in Loch Ness, Scotland; Lake Champlain on the Canada-United States border; and Lake Khaiyr in eastern Siberia are all claimed to have a bulky body, flipperlike limbs, an extremely long neck, and small, stubby head.

Witnesses claim that these prehistoric sea creatures made it through the terrible period of extinction at the end of Cretaceous times. The proof they offer is the remarkable similarity between the fossil evidence of a plesiosaur's flippers and the limbs they claim to have seen with their own eyes on these modern creatures.

Their case is further strengthened by the discovery of the existence of a fish that was thought to have died out with the dinosaurs. A coelacanth, caught off the coast of South Africa in 1938, was the exact replica of fossils that had been dug up previously. Experts claim this species can be no younger than 60 million years in age. The specimen, described as being 5 feet (1.5 m) long with bulging fins and covered in blue-gray scales, was immediately recognized by Madagascan fishermen, who said they often caught such fish.

No one is yet certain whether gigantic throwbacks to prehistoric times really do exist in remote corners of Earth's lakes and seas.

GLOSSARY

ammonites — extinct, soft-bodied aquatic creatures that had tentacles and hard, coiled shells.

beached — washed up or driven onto the beach or shore.

belemnites — extinct marine animals that resembled squids.

buoyant — able to float on water or rise to the surface of water.

clutch (n) — a nest of eggs; a brood, or group of young recently hatched from eggs.

contemporaries — individuals living at the same time.

Cretaceous times — the final era of the dinosaurs, lasting from 144-65 million years ago.

crocodilians — animals belonging to the crocodile family.

cryptozoologists — scientists who study evidence that creatures such as the Loch Ness monster may exist.

devoured — ate quickly or in a greedy way.

elusive — hard to catch; tending to escape.

flippers — broad, flat limbs used for swimming.

flukes — the flattened parts of the tail of a marine animal, such as those of a whale.

foliage — the leaves of a tree, shrub, or plant.

foray (n) — a raid or trip into an area in search of something.

forelimbs — the front arms, legs, fins, or wings of an animal.

fossilized — embedded and preserved in rocks, resin, or other material.

gaping — opened widely, like a yawning mouth.

hadrosaurs — members of a group of duck-billed dinosaurs.

ichthyosaurs — extinct marine reptiles that had fishlike bodies and long snouts.

Jurassic times — the middle era of the dinosaurs, lasting from 213-144 million years ago.

marine — of or relating to the sea or ocean.

modifications — changes in an organism caused by environmental conditions.

mollusks — invertebrates, such as clams and snails, with hard shells; shellfish.

mosasaurs — large, prehistoric marine reptiles that had muscular bodies and very sharp teeth. Mosasaurs became extinct at the same time as the dinosaurs.

nothosaurs — prehistoric marine reptiles from the Triassic era.

paleontology — the study of past geologic periods as they are known from fossil remains.

placodonts — Triassic reptiles, some of which were armored, that lived both on land and in the sea.

plesiosaurs — long-necked, prehistoric, marine reptiles.

pliosaurs — large, prehistoric marine reptiles that had huge jaws and spiked teeth.

predators — animals that hunt other animals for food.

sauropod — a member of a group of plant-eating dinosaurs, such as **Apatosaurus**, mainly from Jurassic times.

slither — to move by sliding along a surface.

teemed — filled to overflowing; swarmed or abounded.

Triassic times — the first era of the dinosaurs, lasting from 249-213 million years ago.

tyrant — a powerful and absolute ruler.

unearthed — dug out of the ground; discovered.

MORE BOOKS TO READ

Creatures of Long Ago: Dinosaurs. Jane Buxton, Editor (National Geographic Society)

Dinosaurs. Andrew Haslam (World Book/Two-Can)

Dinosaurs: Monster Reptiles of a Bygone Era. Secrets of the Animal World (series). Eulalia García (Gareth Stevens)

Dinosaurs and How They Lived. Steve Parker (Dorling Kindersley)

Dinosaurs of the Land, Sea, and Air. Michael Teitelbaum (Rourke Enterprises)

Graveyards of the Dinosaurs: What It's Like to Discover Prehistoric Creatures. Shelley Tanaka (Hyperion Books for Children)

The New Dinosaur Collection (series). (Gareth Stevens)

Prehistoric Marine Reptiles. Judy A. Massare (Franklin Watts)

Raptors, Fossils, Fins and Fangs: A Prehistoric Creature Feature. Ray Troll (Tricycle Press)

World of Dinosaurs (series). (Gareth Stevens)

VIDEOS

Did Comets Kill The Dinosaurs? (Gareth Stevens)

Digging Dinosaurs. (PBS Video)

Dinosaurs. (Smithsonian Video)

Dinosaurs and Other Prehistoric Animals. (Seesaw Video)

Dinosaurs: Remains to Be Seen. (Public Media)

Dinosaurs and Strange Creatures. (Concord Video)

The Nature of the Beast. (PBS Video)

WEB SITES

www.blackhills.com/museum/pliosaur.htm

www.clpgh.org/cmnh/discovery/

www.dinodon.com/index.html

www.dinofish.com/

www.dinosauria.com/

www.ZoomDinosaurs.com

Due to the dynamic nature of the Internet, some web sites stay current longer than others. To find additional web sites, use a reliable search engine with one or more of the following keywords to help you locate more information about dinosaurs. Keywords: *coelacanth, dinosaurs, fossils, paleontology, pliosaur, prehistoric.*

INDEX